T0208851

401(k)-
THE
PATH
TO A
PROSPEROUS
RETIREMENT

401(k)-

THE
PATH
TO A
PROSPEROUS
RETIREMENT

Avoid the Traps.
Find the Money.

VIVIAN R. MCDOUGLE

401(K)—THE PATH TO A PROSPEROUS RETIREMENT AVOID THE TRAPS. FIND THE MONEY.

iUniverse books may be ordered through booksellers or by contacting:

iUniverse
1663 Liberty Drive
Bloomington, IN 47403
www.iuniverse.com
1-800-Authors (1-800-288-4677)

Because of the dynamic nature of the Internet, any web addresses or links contained in this book may have changed since publication and may no longer be valid. The views expressed in this work are solely those of the author and do not necessarily reflect the views of the publisher, and the publisher hereby disclaims any responsibility for them.

Any people depicted in stock imagery provided by Thinkstock are models, and such images are being used for illustrative purposes only. Certain stock imagery © Thinkstock.

ISBN: 978-1-4917-7723-7 (sc)
ISBN: 978-1-4917-7724-4 (e)

Library of Congress Control Number: 2015914766

Print information available on the last page.

iUniverse rev. date: 10/30/2015

Contents

Preface

I first became interested in writing this book when my son started looking for a place to invest the money he had accumulated in his 401K. He spent three years seeking the safety and growth he felt he needed for his funds to last his family's lifetime. He, in my opinion, made excellent choices.

I worked briefly for a mutual fund family in the early 1980's and I have been interested in the stock market since that time. My son would call me and talk about what he found out. There were not many people he knew that had any knowledge of the stock market, so I got to listen while he talked about it. He wanted to know if it sounded reasonable, or if he was overlooking something. He knew, of course, that I wished him and his family the very best.

I have had a tremendous amount of help and encouragement from family and friends in setting up book templets, finding web sites, sending me items that they knew would be an important part of this book, and help in editing to name a few and I greatly appreciate all the help.

In this book I am using information that I acquired during my son's search for a place to put his 401K funds, my training as a representative to sell mutual funds, hours of research, the many items sent to me by friends and family, and the IRS publication 590.

I used the Tables for Compound Interest, and the Compound Interest Accumulation that were used before personal computers were in use. I have included the tables that I used. They are in the back of the book. There are many sites on the internet that would compute this for you, but I think it's interesting to see the multiples in these tables.

These multiples are based on the "The rule of 72" theory which is to divide the rate of return into 72 and that is how many years it would take for your investment to double. This is also known as "compound interest," which is interest drawing interest. I have heard it referred to as "The Eighth Wonder of the World."

I have used 8% as the average rate of return. At 8% your initial investment would double in 9 years. Some financial advisors are beginning to use 10%. The 10% return would double your initial investment in a little over 7 years. You can see what a difference in rate of return would be, but you need to keep in mind the safety factor as well. The market does not give the same rate of return every year, but over the last 30 years it has averaged out to be about 8%. Some years, such as 2008, no mutual fund earned a profit, but in the following years many funds had gains well into the double digits. You can see that this is set up to be a long term investment.

This book is not to tell you where to invest, but to give you the information you need to make these decisions for yourself, what to look for when selecting a mutual fund, and to know what to listen for when using an advisor or a money manager.

Retirement

Do you have dreams of enjoying your golden years by pursuing a hobby that you haven't had time for, while working, or maybe just setting the alarm for another hour of sleep and enjoying a second cup of coffee while leisurely reading the newspaper? Whatever your dreams are, a 401K or an IRA could make this happen.

The potential for accumulating wealth is fantastic. If a person at age 25 invested $300 per mo. Until age 65 and it grew at an 8% rate, using the compound interest table at the end of the book, would have accumulated $1,007,211.00, with a match of $1.00 for $2.00, the young person would have invested a total of $96,000, tax free, over a working lifetime to accumulate over

ONE MILLION DOLLARS.

The number of 401K million dollar households doubled from 2012 to 2014. If he had not invested in the 401K he would have paid $9,600.00 more in federal income taxes, assuming a 10% income tax rate, actually he has only invested $86,400.

The good news is millions people have these 401K accounts and more are signing up every day. The bad news is that it has been estimated that 80% of those account holders have no idea how the stock market works. Many of these account holders are using these accounts as emergency funds, and robbing them when they see money in the account, that they can get their hands on.

The news media is partly to blame for this. They would have you believe that you lost 50% of your savings, during the market fall in 2008. If you were invested in good funds and did not sell at the bottom, you didn't lose it. Most of these funds are invested in businesses that have real value.

I want to tell you the main things to look for and where to find them. Their share prices will fluctuate as the traders rush in to buy or sell. A down market is not necessarily a bad thing, it gives the money managers opportunity to buy some shares below their true market value, and if you are putting money in, this money would buy shares at a lower price. So much hype you see on TV is aimed at traders, not investors.

Wall Street has what they call market makers. Their job is to keep the market moving. If the market stops going up, the traders sell in large number, therefore the market turns and start going down, and by the same method if it stops going down, they start buying in large quantities. Vast numbers of day traders jump into the market, trying to make a little profit on the stock movement.

How Does the Stock Market Work

The market is made up of many companies. As businesses grow and want to expand, they offer stock shares on the market. This is called IPO's (Initial Public Offering). These shares are bought by traders and investors. The companies that sell shares on the stock exchange have to issue a financial report every quarter. An estimation of the profit or loss will come out before the company report is filed. If the actual profit is lower than the estimate, there will be a rash of short sales (sale of stock they do not own) by traders. The share price of the stock will decline. If the profit is higher than the estimate, traders will run the stock up. A lot of this activity will come from traders buying to cover their short sales. The actual value will not change very much.

When stocks get overpriced, stock prices begin to fall. The prices will continue to fall below their actual value. This gyration will make the opportunities for investors to add to their investments at bargain prices. This is good for the investors. They can add to their holding when prices are low, and take profits when stock are overpriced.

Many traders are buying and selling trying to make money on the short term trades. They watch volume of trades and if they think the market is going up they buy. If they see the market going down they sell. If they sell and don't own any shares, this is called short sales. At some point they must buy shares to cover the short sales. The market can change directions very suddenly. The market can change directions several times in one day. This is very risky.

Mutual fund Investors look for shares that are not overpriced. They look to buy shares in companies that have potential for growth. Investors look at P/E (price to earnings ratio), Debt/Net worth ratio, and many other things, in order to find stocks with real value.

Knowledgeable investors keep some cash on hand for 2 major reasons:

1. To be able to buy more shares if the stock price falls below the actual book value and it is deemed to be a solid company.
2. To have money for withdrawals without having to sell shares at a bad time.

There are more than 300 things that can cause a stock to go down in price. To name a few: weather, politics, supply and demand, foreign markets, media hype, etc. This is why it's safer to use a mutual fund if you are investing for your retirement. Let their teams of highly trained professionals work for you.

When the market is in an upward trend, it is called a Bull Market. A trend can last for an indefinite period. Even when it is a Bull Market, there will be small downturns. These are called corrections. A bull market (up-trend) ends when stocks have gotten significantly overpriced. This is called a bubble. A Bear Market (down-trend) is usually a rapid decline, such as we had in 2008. There was a huge drop in a few days. The people who panicked and sold their stock took terrible losses. The mutual funds that were in value funds, were able to buy shares at a reduced price and came out ahead after the market stabilized and began its return to its true value.

Following a sharp downturn, many mutual funds may have double digit earnings for several years.

What Is a 401K

The 401K is the best program ever. It is a program that was put into law in the early 1980s that allows people with earned income to invest for retirement at work. This is very helpful for people who do not have large amounts of money to invest. The 401K encourages the age old way to gain security by saving part of every paycheck. It is designed to allow the average employee to save enough to have a comfortable retirement with little effort on his part. And it permits employees to save by making a deduction from their income go into the 401K account.

The 401K program allows for the employer to contribute to the employee's account, generally matching one dollar for each two dollars taken from the employee's paycheck. Usually the employer match is up to 6%. This money is put in a mutual fund, picked by the employee from several choices that are offered, The employer does not own this money and cannot access any of it. It belongs to the employee.

The employee is not taxed on federal or state income as it goes into your saving, but the money will be taxed as earned income when it is taken out of the fund. A few companies match dollar for dollar up to 6%. You are allowed to put extra money above the company match if you are not in a high income bracket which would be based on your income tax filing status. If you are in a bracket over this amount, you may still be eligible for a partial 401K. The IRS may change this, usually upward, so if you are in this bracket, you should check IRS pub.580 or consult a CPA.

This money is to be left in this account until you reach age 59½. If you take it out sooner, you will have to pay 10% penalty and income tax. There are exceptions to this rule, but if you take money out, you lose the growth on that amount, which is significant over a period of years. At age 70½ you're required to take money out. This is called (RMD) Required Minimum Distribution It is based on your life expectancy as defined by the government.

Most companies have terminated their company retirement plans in favor of the 401K. The 401K has the potential of being better because of these three important factors:

1. The 401K should grow into a large sum over a long period of time.
2. Pensions pay the same amount over your retirement lifetime. If you needed extra money in your retirement years, it would not be available.
3. The 401K money is yours by taking it out in small percentages during your retirement years, and added to your social security it should last over your lifetime,

allowing you to live comfortably and leave a significant estate for your family.

Many pension funds require you to have a certain amount of time (usually 10 years) with the company before you are fully vested. With a 401K all the money that goes into this fund belongs to YOU. If you change jobs you may be able to leave it in the same fund, or you can roll it over into an IRA. Very few people stay in one job over a lifetime.

What Is a Mutual Fund

A mutual fund is an investment company that has huge amounts of money that belongs to the investor that is invested and managed for the investor. They are able to buy large quantities of stocks in many different companies. They are regulated by the Securities Exchange Commission (SEC). Funds are required to have shares in many different companies for safety. This is called diversification. If one company goes broke, they do not lose a large percent of their capital.

The fund price per share rises and falls with the market. The funds pass their profits to the investors through capital gains (selling shares for more than the purchase price) and dividends, which are used to buy more shares.

A mutual fund is run by a fund manager. He or she has a team of assistants that analyze and investigate companies that are strong and look promising. If you are in mutual funds, you have highly trained people working for you.

All mutual funds are not the same; there are two major types:

1. Load Funds: These funds have a sales charge. It can be a front load or a back load. The back load would have the

possibility of being a greater cost, because you would be paying a percentage on the earnings as well as the principal. These funds are usually sold at brokerage houses, banks, or by sales people called "Mutual Fund Representatives".

2. No load Fund: They do not have a sales charge. They can be purchased by contacting the Fund Family.

Both types will have an expense ratio, 1% or lower is reasonable. This expense is deducted before the rate of growth is figured.

There are many good families of funds. The three largest are:

1. Fidelity (the largest)
2. Vanguard (the oldest)
3. T. Rowe Price (the third in size)

There are many different stock groups; large caps, small cap, dividend, growth & income, foreign stock, and emerging markets to name a few. It's no wonder that the general public is confused.

Then there are the sector funds. They only invest in one type of funds. They diversify into many separate companies, but if one type is outpacing all other types of investments, it can't go on indefinitely and will collapse.

Examples top winners by decades:

1940's	Oil stocks
1950's	Electronics
1960's	Leisure time industries, baby products
1970's	Market plunge
1980's	Industrial and technology
1990's	Financial and technology
2000's	Housing
2010's	Oil stocks

If you are tied in to a specific sector group, you are not really diversified. Remember the collapse of the housing market in the late 2000s.

Do I Need a 401K

The answer is YES if you depend on earned income for living expenses and you expect to retire and live comfortably. Social security benefits are only about 30% of your income. They may be a little more if you have a low income, but less if your income is high. Can you imagine living on that? You have a choice to either take a small amount from your salary, or choose to never be able to retire.

Many employees are trying to find ways to gain wealth. Some are investing in business enterprise, some in real-estate, and other things. All of these require large cash or credit amounts. There is a lot of risk involved in these types of investments. Fund your 401K first. It cannot be taken away from you in case of bankruptcy, as the law stands now. Because a mutual fund is diversified, it is much safer than investing in one thing.

Choosing a strong mutual fund is safer than investing in company stock. If the company goes bankrupt, you have not only lost your job, but also your savings. This happened at Enron, a very large company that was claiming to be profitable when it wasn't. Many of their workers had invested their 401K's in the company stock. When the company went under they lost their retirement savings and their jobs.

Here is an example of what a 401K could mean to you:

I will use $3600.00 per year starting at age 25. $1200 of this is company money and your $2400 is tax exempt from federal and state income taxes. I am using 8% as a growth rate because it has been estimated that stocks have had an 8% growth for years. I am beginning to see that 10% growth is being used by some popular financial advisors. Each additional percentage is significant. We know that no one earns the same amount over a lifetime.

This example can be adapted to your situation by using the Compound Interest Accumulation table at the back of the book. If you do not participate, you are actually turning down a 3% raise or the amount of the match.

1. At age 25 you put $200.00 per month, and your employer add $100.00 to that, it amount to $3600.00 per year. At age 65
   $3600.00 x 279.781 = $1,007,211.60

2. At age 30, using the same amounts you could have
   $3,600 x 186.102 = $669,967.20

3. At age 35 with 30 years until retirement
   $3,600. X 122.386 = $$440,589.60

4. At age 40 with 25 years until retirement
   $3,600. X 78.954 = $284,234.40

This shows you what you could accomplish by starting early. You may not need a MILLION to retire on. If you live in an area that has lower taxes and are debt free your living expenses will be much lower. These are things that you need to consider.

Finding the Money

If you think you cannot afford to put money in a 401K think again, you cannot wait to get started. You need to get started NOW.

Most people can find leaks in their budget. You should look at the spending plan later listed in this book. Look for leaks on the flexible spending.

- Look at bank overdraft charges. This is money for nothing. Banks make a lot of money off of overdrafts. Get a cash back credit card. Be sure you pay the entire bill before the due date each month.

- Beware of high interest charges. Most retail stores are charging 25% or more on credit purchases. They also charge late fees. I've seen late fees as high as $29.00. Late charges also have a negative effect your credit score.

- Guard your credit history. A low credit score (FICO) will have a negative influence on other things in your life, such as a higher rate of interest in buying large items. Also it may affect your being considered for a job, or even renting an apartment.

- Look at eating out. A family of four can eat the same or better food at home for about what a meal for one out would cost when eating out. Eating out should be a special occasion. If you eat out regularly, it gets to be boring.

- Taking your lunch to work will save considerably, and may be healthier than going out to eat, even at a fast food café you will spend $8.00 or more.

- Try taking meat and cheese sandwiches, with a piece of fruit and a cookie, or a can of soup to eat with a sandwich. Be creative, you will be surprised at what you come up with. You may have leftovers from the evening meal that would make a good lunch. Most work places have refrigerators and microwave ovens.

- By taking your lunch, you are saving on car expense, frustration of finding a parking place, getting served, and back to work on time.

- Bottled water: Water is healthy and everywhere you go you see people with these bottles, but it runs into needless spending. If you cannot drink tap water, buy a gallon of filtered water, not distilled water. A gallon of this water will cost about $1.00, and will give you about 18 bottles. That is some savings.

- Shop once a week for food, with a list. A little planning can save money. When making your list don't forget to consult the grocery advertisements.

- Some of these may ideas may sound extreme to you, but do you want to BE WEALTHY, or to LOOK WEALTHY? If you look around you, you will see others doing these things. One person told me it is fun to get a bargain. When it becomes more fun to save money that spend it, you will be well on your way to becoming a millionaire.

- All successful companies have purchasing agents. Take an idea from them and consider yourself a purchasing agent. Anticipate your needs ahead of time. Compare prices and watch for sales. After July 4th and December 31st there will be lots of sales. Garage sales, estate sales and moving sales are excellent places to look for things you are looking to buy. Don't buy more than you need.

- When your car is becoming unreliable and you are in the market for a new car, consider a used one. The car rental companies change out their fleets about every two years. These will be good late model cars with low mileage. Be sure to consult the "Blue Book" for appropriate pricing. When you find a car that you want to buy, get the serial number and check it out on the internet by using "CARFAX". You will get a report on that car showing any problems it may have had.

You are less likely to get a lemon this way than if you bought a new one. You could expect to get a late model used car financed for 36 months for about what your payment would be for a new car financed for 60 months.

Take good care of your car and drive it as long as it is dependable.

If you use these methods, you will not only have enough to finance a great retirement, but also have money for other things that make life enjoyable.

When setting up a spending plan, be sure to use your take home pay. The important thing is to know where your money is going. If you are a couple it is important to plan together

Which Fund Should I Choose

Your employer will give you several funds to choose from. There are many ways to make this decision.

There are many sites on the internet that can help you. Several years ago, when I was in an Investment Club, one of the members introduced us to Yahoo Finance. It has been my favorite since that time. I believe you will find that this site is easy to use.

Make a list of the stock symbols that you have been given to choose from.

1. Go to Yahoo Finance on the internet and hit enter. Then click on Business Finance, Stock market.
2. Put this on your favorite list.
3. Enter your first fund symbol.

This will give you some current information about the fund. Look on the left side of the screen. You will find numerous headings. Look for the following and enter each separately:

- BASIC CHART

  Enter one of the symbols, then enter next fund symbol and click on compare. Continue to enter each symbol until you have all of them on the chart. This will show you which had the best run. Look for the one that had the least decline in the '08 meltdown, and which one recovered sooner.

- PROFILE

  Enter each fund symbol separately. This site will tell you quite a bit about the fund. The Morning Star rating the stars are from 1 to 5, with 5 being the safest in its category. It will show the manager's name and his experience, fees and expenses, compared to category average, and also turnover rate.

- RISK

  This page gives the Morning star rating. In this case the lower number is considered safer. It will tell you how many years the fund was up and how many years it was down. All funds have had down years. It also tells you the best year and the worst year.

- HOLDINGS

  This page shows the name of the top ten companies that the fund has the highest percent of investment in. You will notice that they have a very small percentage of investment in each. This shows they are well diversified, as required by the SEC. This information may not be current, as they list it every quarter, and it takes about a month to get it on the internet.

Trap Number One

Trap number one is not getting started. Here are a few examples, to show this.

You at age 25 will have 40 years to invest, using $2400.00 per year with a company match of $1200.00 and that would equal $3600 per year going into your 401K.

- At 40 years multiply $3600. X 279.781 = $1,007,211
- At 35 years multiply $3600 X 186.102 = $669,967
- At 30 years multiply 3600 X 122.346 = $440,446
- At 25 years multiply 3600 X 78.954 = $284,234
- At 20 years multiply 3600 X 49.423 = $177,923

As you can see, it is important to start early.

Don't give up if you are older, you can invest larger amounts and still have a good retirement.

The 401K is a do it yourself plan, for yourself. If you depend on earned income, and do not have a pension, you need this in order to retire. If you have a job that you enjoy and still want to work, that is fine, but I'm seeing a lot of older people working because Social Security isn't enough to live on. There are a lot of homeless people, some of whom said that they had good jobs, but didn't save anything.

Don't get caught in this trap

The 401K really works. I am seeing some retirees on this program and they say they have more discretionary income than they had when they were employed, and are enjoying retirement without having to lower their standard of living. Way to go!

What Is an IRA

IRA stands for individual retirement account. There are two kinds; the traditional IRA and a Roth IRA. The individuals must set up these accounts for themselves. There will be many agents out there to assist you, but you need to know how to evaluate the funds, so you can know if they are right for you.

Some restrictions apply for very high earners. You can have an IRA even if you have a 401K .

If married, your spouse may also have an IRA even though the spouse does not have an income as long as one of you has enough income to cover it.

The traditional IRA permits you to invest up to $5,500 per year, if you have that much in earned income, and deduct it from your income on your tax for the year. If you are age 50 or older you may put an extra $1,000 for a total of $6,500 a year. The IRS may change these amounts, but the amounts are usually increased when changed. This money will not be taxed as it is invested, but will be taxed as earned income when you withdraw the funds. If you withdraw funds from this account before you reach age 59 1/2, you will be charged a 10% penalty and income tax on it.

After age 59 ½, you may take out as much or as little as you want, and the amount will be counted as earned income for income tax purposes. At age 70½ you will be required to take the money out based on life expectancy. This is called Required Minimum Distribution (RMD). If you do not take the required amount out there will be 50% excise tax on the amount not withdrawn that year. You will be allowed to take out as much as you want, but you must take the minimum or above or pay a heavy penalty.

You are eligible to open an IRA account even if you have a retirement plan at work. However, it may be phased out if you are a high income earner. If you are in a high income bracket, check Internal Revenue Service publication 590 or talk with your CPA.

What Is a Roth IRA

The difference in a Roth IRA and the traditional IRA is that the Roth fund in not tax deferred. You are not exempt from income tax. You pay income tax when you put funds into it. When you take the money out after reaching the age of 59 ½ you do not owe tax on income on the original amount or on the earnings.

You may take out what you've invested at any time without penalty however, you may not take out the earnings without paying a penalty on it. If you take the earnings out before age 59 ½, you will be charged a 10% penalty. There is no required minimum distribution.

This is good if you expect to live a long life.

As the law stands now, you may roll over funds from your 401K. This rolled over amount must be left in the Roth for 5 years before you can withdraw the amount rolled over without penalty.

With the conventional IRA, the RMD withdrawal requirement, you may not have enough money for extra needs as you reach the upper 80's and beyond. The Roth could still be increasing in value, while you would be required to take money out the traditional IRA.

Another good reason for the Roth is after you have invested in 401K up to the amount the company matches, it may be wise to invest in a Roth IRA instead of an education account, because Roth, being a retirement account, it will not be counted against your students if applying for a grant or needs based scholarship as the law stands now. Also, if your child needs help, you could pull money out of the Roth that you had put in, but not the growth, without penalty.

There are some educational benefits also. The educational fund part has many restrictions. The laws change frequently, so check carefully before making a decision on this.

You might start a Roth IRA for a child that is working part time. A gift from parents or grandparents could be used, up to the amount the child earned. The growth on this should be significant. Since the gift giver cannot deduct it from his income the Roth would be a good way to go.

A one way to choose a mutual fund for your Roth IRA, is through a financial publication.

There are many good ones on the market. Early in the year go to the public library or to a newsstand and look for a magazine that has rated the major funds. Some of them will have hundreds of mutual funds along with their trading symbols and other in that I found to be very useful as follows:

The name of the company, their trading symbol and the annualized return for:

- One year
- Three-years
- Five-years
- Ten-years

The ten-year is very important because it includes the sharp decline in 2009. It will give you an idea of which funds did the best under bad circumstances.

Some of these publications will also give you the:

- Sales load, if any
- Yearly expense
- Total assets
- Telephone numbers fund of the company

After studying this, choose several and check them out on Yahoo Finance, as instructed in the chapter "How to Choose a Fund for your 401K." After you have made a decision, call the fund company you have chosen and ask them to send you the paperwork to get you started.

This form will give him authority to invest your funds. You will be asked to designate a beneficiary and a contingent beneficiary. In case of your death, this fund will not go through probate; it will go directly to the beneficiary, if you choose a person or persons.

You will be asked to have a monthly amount drafted from your bank account and added to your Roth, or you may send additional funds in a lump sum. A good time to do this would be after you get a tax refund.

Some brokers encourage you to buy individual stocks for your traditional or Roth IRA. It would be almost impossible to diversify with small amounts every month. Your commission would eat up your profits. Unless you are highly trained in investments, this is very risky.

There are some companies that sell programs that tell you that you can know when to buy and when to sell. I have seen a couple of these programs. They are for traders not investors. They go by volume of sales more than value. A stock can turn around several times a day.

Watch for sales pitches saying this may be the next BIGGIE. Usually these are startup companies that are trying to get working capital. Most of these are low priced stock. They are referred to as "Pump and Dump." If it isn't making a profit it's a high risk. A large percent of startup companies fail. If you are tempted to try these offers use your Las Vegas money not your IRA retirement fund!

Trap Number Two

Taking money out of your retirement account is a big mistake! For example, you at age 40 wanted to know if you should take your money out of your 401K in order to eliminate some of your debt.

You started a retirement savings at age 30.

Still using the same formula at 6% of your salary and 3% of the company match at age 40 that would amount to:

$3,600×15.645 = $56,000

That's a lot of money but there would be a 10% penalty and it would likely put you in a higher tax bracket which at this time is 39 ½. Zip! Half of it is gone.

Starting over you would have 25 years to invest:

$3,600 year for 25 years
$3,600 x 78.954 = $284,262

If you hadn't taken the money, out at age 65 you would've had the following:

$3,600 x 186.102 equal $669,967

$669,967 – $ 284.262 = $385,705 A big loss!

If you take out the $56,304 at age 40, you will have $385,705 less in your retirement account at age 65. In other words, you would have traded $28,000 now for approximately $385,000 at age 65.

Remember this money cannot be taken from you, even in bankruptcy. Do not take the money out. Look for other ways to work your money problems out.

What If I Have Changed Jobs

You could leave your 401K where it is. If you have checked out the fund that you have your 401K in and it is a good one you may want to leave it where it is. Be sure to keep the latest report you have on it, or you could roll it over into a traditional IRA. If you decide to roll it over go back to Yahoo Finance and use it to find a good mutual fund. Have the fund company send you the paperwork that will allow them to make the transfer. This is called a rollover.

A rollover is much easier than taking the money out of the present 401K. The 401K fund would be required to deduct income tax on it. You would have 60 days to make the transfer, but you would have to pay the amount deducted in cash or reduce your IRA by the amount taxed.

Will I Be Able to Retire

Age 50 is a good time for a financial checkup. You should be at about your earnings peak, the children should be independent, and it's time to get serious about your retirement. Take a look at your net worth and decide if you are on track to retire. First, estimate how much money you will need to retire without limiting your lifestyle. To do this you should go over your expected expenses as follows:

List of fixed expenses:

- Housing cost $_____
- Utilities $_____
- Insurance $_____
- Taxes $_____
- Installment payments $_____
- Other $_____
  Total $_____

Estimate your flexible expenses

- Food $_____
- Clothing $_____
- Transportation $_____

- Personal-care $_____
- Recreation $_____
- Contributions $_____
- Other $_____
  Total $_____

Total your fixed expenses and your flexible expenses and this is the amount you will need to retire comfortably.

Look at your home mortgage if you have one. If you have more years left on it than you have years until retirement, check on refinancing. Most mortgage rates are low. Look at consumer debt and see if you can get it paid off before retirement.

Using the same example starting at age 30, having invested 3,600 year and 8% return this would be an estimate of the amount you would have at retirement:

$3,600 x 49.423 = $177,922 at age 50

Growth on $177,922 for 15 years at age 65 would be

$177,922 × 3.172 = $564,371

Plus the accumulation for the next 15 years

$3,600 × 29.324 = $105,566
$564,371 + $105,566 = $669,937

Perhaps you did not start your investment at age 30 and were contributing a different amount.

Use the 3.172 to see how much it would increase in 15 years and use the amount you are contributing each year multiplied by 29.334.

You may need to increase your contributions, and try to retire your debts. You have another 15 years to do this. If you decide you want more saved for retirement, using example $800,000, then one way to get an estimate is to go to Google and enter:

www.calculator.net/investment-calculator.html

Entry for target	800,000
Entry for years	15
Starting principle	177,923
Average rate of return	8%
Click on calculator monthly	698.00
Already investing:	$ 300 per month

Increase needed to reach the target of $398 per month.

You might consider putting this extra amount in a Roth IRA. It would be taxed going into the fund, but would be tax exempt when it's taken out. You would not have to withdraw it at age 70 ½ as required by the traditional IRA.

If you live a long life and need extra medical funds it would be there. The traditional IRA has to be withdrawn based on life expectancy and would be greatly reduced at an older age. This Roth could be used for long-term care.

Sales people are pushing long term care insurance. If you invested the $398 each month into a Roth IRA until age 65 and left it invested until age 75 using 8% percent return, this is what you would have:

Example:

- $398 ×12 = $4,776.00 per year
- $4776.00 × 29.324 = $139,263.33 at age 65
- $139,263.33 × 2.159 = $300,611.24 at age 75

This money, in a Roth account, could be used for assisted living as well as nursing care or anything you needed. The Roth would continue to earn on the amount not used. If you decide to do this, it would be advisable to take money from the traditional IRA first.

I have personally known two people who had nursing home insurance.

One had a long illness and used up all the funds that the long-term care provided and still needed money. The other one had a short illness and never used her long-term care insurance that she had paid on for years.

The Roth seems to me to be a wonderful alternative. Each person's health needs differ. Many people are living well into their 90's.

I recently heard a suggestion that recommended the use of term life insurance for long-term care for a married couple, on the theory that when one of the spouses passed away the spouse left would be able to use the insurance to pay nursing home care.

I investigated this possibility and learned that if you were in good health at age 50 you could get a term life policy guaranteed rate for 20 years. After 20 years if you were still in good health at age 70 you could get the policy that would be a significantly higher rate. At age 90 you would no longer be covered by this term life policy. This does not seem to be a good choice. You would pay out more in premiums than you would have invested in the Roth if you lived a long life. Remember you would have to be in good health to get this insurance in the first place.

I am not against term life insurance for young couples with children. It's very affordable at a young age. It insures your family in case of an untimely death.

Age 59½

Retirement is getting closer, are you ready?

It's time to redo your estimate of what you will need each year. Then figure what you will have coming in from Social Security and subtract that amount from the amount you will need. Then you can figure from the previous examples and the tables at the back of the book approximately what your 401K value would be at retirement. Then divide the life expectancy. According to IRS at age 65 life expectancy is 21 years. Divide 21 into your 401K value at 65 and that should give you a pretty good estimate of what you could take out each year.

Example:

You had at age 65 in his 401K:

$669,967 divided by 21 = $31,903

Adding Social Security to that makes it

$31,903 + $14,000 = $45,903

At this time you should be looking for a place to invest your 401K. If you find one that is promising, you could do a roll over at this time without penalty. If you only wanted to put a small amount in and you are considering a money manager, ask if you could roll over, let's say $50,000.

They ordinarily don't take amounts under $250,000.

But, you could ask. If you have a larger amount to invest when you retire, they might be inclined to do so. I have known of this working.

Social Security

Social Security has three major purposes.

1. It provides financial assistance in retirement. It allows you to receive benefits as early as age 62 or you can choose to wait and receive more at a later date up to age 70. At this time your benefit would increase 8% for each year that you delayed payment, from age 62 up to age 70. This decision should be based on your needs and your health. If you have a job that you enjoy, you may be able to work past retirement age and still draw SS. If you are younger than full retirement, and earn above the specified amount, Social Security will deduct $1 for each $2 you earn. This amount changes yearly. Before making any decisions contact your Social Security office to get the current facts, and then make your decision.

2. Disability assistance: If you can prove your claim. The amount of payment is based on the amount and the number of years you were covered.

3. A spouse can draw SS on the deceased spouse's SS. The surviving spouse can start drawing at a reduced rate at

age 60. He or she can also draw on the deceased spouse if there are dependent children under the age of 18.

Social Security also provides health insurance under a program called Medicare. You should apply for this about 3 month before your 65th birthday. There may be extra cost involved if you delay.

There is a web site that been created to give you information on your personal SS account.

Go to "gov/mystatement"

This will provide estimates for your retirement, disability, and survivor benefits.

Getting Ready

You may have changed jobs and left a pension or 401K behind. Ask your former employers to send you a statement of that pension or 401K. If you cannot find former employers, they may have gone out of business or changed their name but you will still have that account in your name. This is your money, be sure to claim it.

For pensions or 401K left behind that you can't locate, go to these government agencies and they will have a record:

- Pension Benefit Guarantee Corp (PBCG)
  or
- National Registry of Unclaimed Benefits (NRURB)

Fraud

Now that you have a large amount of money, the hard part is how to make it last for the rest of your life.

Yes, fraud is alive and well. There are many scams out there. One of the ways they work is that they go into a new location and strike up a friendship with someone they meet. They win that person's confidence and get him to invest and show incredible results over the short term. That person tells his friends and encourages them to invest. The funds are put in the name of the perpetrator or a company that he has started. The rest is history. Your money is gone.

Do not invest in anything that you can't check out on the internet. Never transfer your money to a salesman. Make it payable to a large holding company, and see that it remains in your name where you could check on it daily. If you are promised profits that are unrealistic, that raises a red flag.

Remember Madoff! He had all the investor's money in his name, and he was sending out false reports, all the while siphoning off the profits to increase his own wealthy lifestyle. When the investors began to withdraw their funds, there was not enough money to cover them, and the fraud was uncovered.

Another risky investment is Limited Partnerships. Shares are sold to raise capital for a project. The money is used to finance a project.

If you need the money back, it is may not available until the project is profitable or sold. The controlling partner has the access to all the funds and many times, when payroll is met, there is not any money left. I have known some of these to go bankrupt. Especially in real estate when the economy goes sour as it did in 2008. These were not actually fraud, they were ill timed.

Limited partnerships are illiquid investments. There is more chance of fraud in this type of investment, because your money is co-mingled with all investors and you have no way of checking on it. Proceed with caution.

Oil is another risky limited partnership. It takes a lot of money to drill a well, and if it does not produce there is a big chance the project may go bankrupt. Stick with the big established companies because they can afford the risk.

Beware of unsolicited offers. The hype sounds great. The industry has a name for this, "Pump and Dump." This is used to sell penny stocks. If it is not making a profit, consider it to be very risky. If it sounds too good to be true, and you cannot check it out, walk away.

Be sure to check out anything you are being offered. Never make a hasty decision. If it's a good deal today, it will be a good deal tomorrow. Stay with tried and true investors or funds.

Annuities

There are many different kinds of annuities, and new ones being created every day. When you invest in an annuity you pay a high commission and your return is based on the amount left. Your funds are now the property of the annuity fund.

Here are the major types:

- Life Annuity: It works like a pension fund. It gives you a guaranteed income for life.

- Joint life: Gives a smaller specified amount and the surviving spouse receives the same lifetime specified amount for life.

- Terms of year annuity: You are guaranteed a certain amount for a set number of years. It can be 10, 15, or 20 years. If you die before the term is up, your beneficiary gets to collect for the remaining time. If you live longer than the payout time, sorry, I hope you have other income sources, because this one is gone.

- Variable Annuity: These are sold telling you that your income will not go below a certain amount.

The income is based on stock market return and may not reflect the market growth. It may be based on the daily average closing price.

The annuity funds promoters are very aggressive in their sales approach. They usually have seminars offering free advice and dinner. Then they canvass the group and set up private appointments. Be wary of pressure.

Do not invest out of fear. The more you know about financial opportunities, the better you will be able to make wise decisions. Weigh the information careful. This is a big decision. The sales commission is high and is taken right off of your initial stake.

There are new ones being brought on the market.

Be careful about new funds because they have no history to point to.

PRO: Annuities work like a traditional pension in that you get a check each month.

CON: It works like a pension in that you get a check each month. At your death and, or at your spouse's death, the money goes to the annuities. There is no increase for inflation. Inflation is a real threat.

Financial Planners

Financial Planners have to be licensed. There are several different designations. One is CFP (Certified Financial Planner). Another is CFA (Certified Financial Adviser), and a third one is CHFA (Charter Certified Financial Adviser).

There are web sites that are helpful.

Finra.org

This site has a list of designations and also uses Finra's "Broker Check" to see if they have had any law suits filed against them.

They earn their money in different ways. All who have obtained these licenses have spent hours and hours studying and have passed very rigid tests and also met the ethics requirements. Ask them about their designation. They will be happy to tell you. They have every right to be proud of their achievements.

Two types of Planners include:

1. A Mutual fund Representative: They sell financial products, such as mutual fund shares, limited

partnerships, and insurance. Proceed carefully. There may be a conflict of interest.

2. Fee only planner: Assists and recommends a portfolio of investments suitable to your set of circumstances. Usually these are individual stocks. Then you are left to manage them yourself. They charge an hourly rate. This is called a consulting fee. Most people do not have the ability to make the right decisions about stocks because they let their emotions get in the way. When stocks are going down they sell at the bottom. When stocks are going up, and the huckster are shouting "Buy now," they are inclined to buy at the top.

Money Managers

Money Managers are usually licensed as CFA's but may have other designations as well. Ask; they are proud of these accomplishments.

As the term applies, when you hire a money manager, you give him the power of attorney to make trades with your money. He or she is authorized to make trades in your account for you, and deduct his fee from your account. This is usually done on a quarterly basis, at a set fee. 1% annually is considered reasonable.

Here are some things you need to know:

1. Are you comfortable talking to him? Does he answer your questions directly? If he does not want to discuss it or thinks you wouldn't understand, he is not the broker for you.
2. How does he get his information? Does he believe in value stocks rather than trying to catch the market ups and downs?
3. How long has he been in this business? You want someone who has survived to 2009 stock collapse.

4. How much did his accounts decline in 2009? All had losses in that year.
5. How long did it take for them to recover? If longer than 18 to 24 months that is not a good record.
6. Where will your money be kept? It must be in a large brokerage firm, in your name, where you can check on it on a daily basis. Ask if the brokerage house is insured against fraud. He should know this. They are not insured against market gyrations.

If you like what you have found out, the broker will set up another interview. At that time he should have a portfolio ready to invest. Take your latest info from your 401K or IRA and he will have a rollover form to complete the transaction. Look at it carefully. Be sure that the funds are being sent to a third party brokerage firm in your name.

Tell him how much you want to withdraw each month, and where you want it sent; your bank of course. The brokerage house will not send the check anywhere other than where you have specified. This is a very good way to prevent fraud. If you have an emergency and need more money, you may have to go back and sign another form. It's your money. The brokerage firm issues the check. It doesn't go through the advisor.

This is the way most people with large sums to invest do it. This way you have highly skilled personnel working for you.

Withdrawal Plan

This is also known as a distribution plan. You want this money to last over a long period of time, say 28 years. You will need a plan. A very conservative plan is to withdraw 3% annually. If the market slides during the first year or two you would still have a sizeable amount left. Then you could increase the distribution each year to adjust for inflation. Use the same figures as used earlier, and the fact that you retired at 65.

Example: $669,967.00 x 3% = $20,099.00

Another way would be to take a cue from the Minimum Retirement Distribution that you have to use when you reach 70 ½ years of age with an estimated life expectancy of 28 years.

Example: $669,967.00 divided by 28 =$23,927.00

This added to your social security check at an average of $14,000 a year equals to $37,927.00

This fund should still be growing.

Planners usually advise clients to invest heavily in bonds as they reach retirement age. The theory behind this is; bonds do not fluctuate as much as stocks do. Currently bonds are yielding about half of the amount that stocks will grow. It would make sense to rebalance if you were going to take all the money out at once, but if you are taking a distribution over a long period of time. It seems to me that you would be short changing yourself if you took your money out of stocks and invested it in bonds.

This money is yours and everyone has different needs. This is just an observation, and something you need to discuss with your advisor.

I recently heard of a planner who was telling his client to rebalance every month. The term, rebalance, means to take money from the one growing at a faster rate (the stock) and put it in the one growing slower (bonds) each month. I would call this churning and churning is against the law. When you buy or sell the broker gets a commission. I guess this broker needed the money.

Watch carefully. You want an advisor or broker that is working for your best interest and not more interested in making a commission.

Required Minimum Withdrawal

At age 70½ and each year going forward you will be required to take a Required Minimum Distribution. This is also referred to as RMD. You will be required to take a distribution based on your account balance on December 31st of the previous year, and your life expectancy and the life expectancy of your spouse. This amount will change as your life expectancy changes each year. Your tax preparer will have this information. Also you can find this online. Go to Google and enter:

Uniform lifetime table.

You could also get IRS Publication 590.

If your distribution is not large enough, you will be subjected to a 50% tax on the amount not distributed.

The Required Minimum Distribution cannot be rolled over into a Roth.

The year that you reach 70½ is referred to as the required beginning date. That year you have until April 1st of the following year to take the required minimum distribution. In the years following, you must make the required minimum by Dec

31st. If you wait until after Dec 31st to withdraw the beginning distribution year, you will have to pay income taxes on both amounts in the same year. That might put you in a higher tax bracket.

If you have more than one individual account, the distribution amount required must be computed for each one, but you then have the option of taking the full amount from one account.

For example, if one is earning more than the other, it would be to your advantage to take the distribution out of the account that isn't doing as well and let the better account continue to grow. If one account is an inherited account you must take the required amount out of it separately. You may not comingle an inherited IRA.

Beneficiaries

If the owner died on or before the beginning date for required minimum distribution, figure the required amount as if he had lived all year.

If you are the beneficiary surviving spouse, you may elect to be treated as the owner. The distribution would be made on the owner's life expectancy in the year of his death. In the following years the distribution may be made based on the new owner's (spouse beneficiary) life expectancy.

This is an important consideration, because if you are a surviving spouse beneficiary and you do not elect to be treated as owner, you will not have the protection from creditors that owners have.

If the owner had not reached the age of 59 ½, the spouse may need access to this money and the spouse chooses to be treated as a beneficiary, rather than an owner, he must make annual withdrawals without penalty. He may take more than the required amount if he wishes at any age.

If the owner died after reaching 70 ½, and you are the surviving spouse and elect to be the new owner you generally must base required minimum distribution on the longer of:

- Your single life expectancy or
- The deceased owner's life expectancy.

If you are not a spouse, you will be classified as a beneficiary, if the deceased owner had reached age 70½ at his death, the beneficiary must withdraw:

- On his life expectancy or
- On the life expectancy of the owner; choosing the one that is longer.

If the owner has not reached 70 ½, you will be required to take minimum withdrawals base on your life expectancy. You are not limited to that amount. It is just the minimum.

If you are the beneficiary of a deceased owner, you cannot add to this IRA and you cannot roll over any funds into this account. It must be kept separately from your IRA's and you must take minimum distributions

If there is more than one beneficiary, the IRA must be divided into accounts for each as specified. This must be done by the end of the year following the year in which the owner died. If the account if not divided by September 30, following the year that the owner died, the beneficiary with the shortest life expectancy will be designated the beneficiary.

If you are the beneficiary of a Roth IRA, you are required to take the same distribution as specified as the above traditional IRA. The Roth IRA would not be taxed either state or federal income tax.

Observations

After I began this book, family and friends started giving me stories of their experiences, many I have used. Some of them have been asked to find information for me.

One friend gave me a little book called; "An Uncommon Way to Wealth"

It was written under an assumed name in France in the 1700's. A young man became acquainted with a very wise old man. His question to him was, "How can I obtain wealth?"

The old man gave him lessons on accumulating wealth as follows:

1. Find a job and save something from every paycheck. The ups will average out with the downs. (We call this Dollar Averaging).
2. The rule of 72, the rate of return divided into 72, will determine how long it will take for that money to double. (The old man cited the book "Scales of Commerce" by Willsford, published in 1640, giving Willsford credit for this rule)

3. Understanding diversification. (As Ben Franklin said, "Don't put all of your eggs in one basket.")
4. Rest; give your brain time to digest the information. (Don't make hasty decisions)
5. Seek wisdom and respect the council from experienced experts. (Let the experts work for you)
6. Treat everyone with respect and deal honestly. (Do unto others as you would have them do unto you.)
7. He went on to say, "Few people will follow these rules".

I was amazed to find so many ideas that I was expressing in this book had been used for ages by people searching for wealth. It turns out that the 401K is just a relatively new twist on obtaining wealth. I certainly hope he was wrong on the last comment. The 401K makes it easy to invest, and if the people do not take advantage of it, we are going to have more people living in poverty than we have working in the near future.

Compound Accumulation Table

Accumulation table shows how much a series of payments of $1.00 due at the beginning of the year, will amount to at the end of various years, with interest compounded annually. Use your yearly rate of investment:

Years	6%	8%	9%	10%	12%
5	5.975	6.336	6.523	6.716	7.115
10	13.972	15.645	16.560	17.531	19.655
15	24.673	29.324	32.003	34.950	41.753
20	38.993	49.423	55.765	63.002	80.699
25	58.156	78.954	92.324	108.182	149.334
30	83.802	122.346	148.575	180.943	270.293
35	118.121	186.102	235.125	298.127	483.463
40	164.048	279.781	368.292	486.852	859.142

Compound Interest Table

Lump sum table shows how much $1.00 will amount to at the end of various years with interest compounded annually.

Years	6%	8%	9%	10%	12%
5	1.338	1.469	1.539	1.611	1.762
10	1.791	2.159	2.367	2.594	3.106
15	2.397	3.172	3.642	4.177	5.474
20	3.207	4.661	5.604	6.727	9.646
25	4.292	6.848	8.623	10.835	17.000
30	5.743	10.063	13.268	17.449	29.960
35	7.686	14.785	20.414	28.102	52.800
40	10.286	21.725	31.409	45.259	93.051

Printed in the United States
By Bookmasters